# BORN TO LOSE,

# BUT <u>BOUND</u>

# TO WIN

*An inspirational story
of victory over poverty
and bitterness!*

By

## Anthony Burrus

*Born to Lose, But Bound to Win*
Copyright © 2015 Terri Bonin, Conroe, Texas

SpiriTruth Publishing Company
Your source of discount digital publishing

7710-T Cherry Park Drive, Suite 224
Houston, TX 77095
(713) 766-4272

Eddie@SpiriTruthPublishing.com
http://www.SpiriTruthPublishing.com

Published in the United States of America

EBook: 978-1-312-52125-4
Softcover: 978-1-63443-192-7
Hardcover: 978-1-312-52124-7

# Contents

## Introduction

# THE LIGHT OF DAY

*Far above the night of selfishness*
*That blinds me on my way;*
*I see the path that leads above*
*To the land of the Light of Day.*

*Far above the cry of human flesh*
*I hear the call of He;*
*Who made the way for the Light of Day*
*Who said, "Come, follow me."*

*Above the blood stained fields of battle*
*Where the wars of man ne'er cease;*
*I see a world of brotherhood,*
*of justice, love and peace.*

*Far above the mounts of hate and war,*
*And the racial sandstorms of man;*
*I see the peak of a Mount whose summit*
*Upon which I will someday stand.*

By Reverend Anthony Washington Burrus
(May 1, 1965)

## Chapter One
# A COURSE IS SET

The blistering sun beat mercilessly down on an August day in Castle, Oklahoma, 1934. One could only pray that the wind would come "sweepin' down the plain." But such was not the case. At that time, the population of Castle consisted of a handful of black sharecroppers and their families who lived in small wood frame houses scattered amongst the cotton fields.

Segregation was complete back then. Black folks and white folks had little to do with one another. Blacks were simply dirty property or nuisances to the white landowners. But the white landowners needed them to tend and harvest their crops.

At the Burrus house, five-year-old Anthony sat on the dusty porch when he began to faintly recognize the whine of a police car's siren in the distance. He looked up to identify the blinking lights heading towards his home. There was rarely much excitement around Anthony's home. Life consisted of working in the fields from dawn to dark, so the sound of the siren quickly captured his attention.

He ran inside where his daddy was washing his hands and face in a large ceramic bowl in preparation for dinner. As he dried his hands, he picked Anthony up with a smile and carried him to the front screen door, looking outside.

Dust billowed behind the squad car as it raced up the final stretch of dirt road to the house. Skidding to a stop, the screaming siren wound down, then silenced. Both car doors swung open and two tall uniformed white police officers climbed out, adjusted their gun belts and swaggered up to the front door.

"Burrus," one said gruffly to Anthony's daddy, "where are your boys, Bob and Bill?"

Mr. Burrus stepped outside. Placing little Anthony down, he answered, "I don't know, officer."

Sarcastically one of them said, "Where are the molasses you stole from Johnson's farm?"

"Officer, I don't know nothin' about no molasses," Mr. Burrus replied.

"Yes you do, Burrus. You're the one who stole 'em, ain't you?" the officer insisted.

"No sir." Anthony's daddy answered calmly. "I didn't steal no one's molasses."

After a second, then third attempt to get Mr. Burrus to confess to the theft, the officers then looked at Anthony.

"Boy, come here," one growled belligerently. Tiny Anthony dressed in nothing but a long-tailed shirt, stood frozen with fear, staring at those angry white policemen. He'd hardly ever seen a white person, and no one had ever talked to him like that.

"I said git over here, boy!" the officer shouted.

Cautiously, Anthony obeyed and walked toward the demanding officer. At that moment, each officer pulled his service revolver, cocked and leveled it at little Anthony's head—touching his skull.

Mr. Burrus was totally caught off guard. There was nothing he could do. Both he and his baby boy's lives were in danger. One wrong word could end in disaster.

"Anthony?" His eyes were like saucers. With a pounding heart and clammy palms, the boy trembled from head to toe. Those big white police officers looked like giants to him. He had never been threatened before. He was just a baby.

"Boy, look at me. Your daddy stole Mr. Johnson's molasses, didn't he?"

Tongue-tied, Anthony was much too frightened to speak.

The officer yelled louder, "I said, *Did your daddy steal Mr. Johnson's molasses!?*"

"Yes sir, yes sir," Anthony replied fearfully.

With that the two men turned, holstered their guns, and handcuffed his daddy. They drug him from the porch to the car, crammed him into the back seat, and slammed the door. Anthony and his mother watched in terror from the window as the police car sped back down the dirt road until it disappeared in a cloud of dust.

Mr. Burrus was charged with theft and concealing stolen property. He went before a judge and was sentenced to one year in the state penitentiary at McAlister, Oklahoma.

● ● ●

Hello, my name is Anthony Burrus. It was my daddy who was taken from our family for an entire year in 1934. It was those two white police officers who planted seeds of hatred for the white race in my five-year-old heart; seeds that would later bring a harvest of bitterness, anger, fear, and distrust of whites.

This book is the story of how I was delivered from the prison of bitterness, hatred and unforgiveness into the palace of freedom and liberty in Christ Jesus--to love and to be loved.

10

## Chapter Two

# A HUMBLE BEGINNING

C ome with me if you will to another world, a world that you likely know not of. It is a world from which I came; for I am the 14th child of a family with 26 children. More about that in a moment, but first...

My grandfather was bought and sold as a slave in Tennessee's Cumberland Mountain range; a beautiful stretch of mountains that reaches from Virginia, through West Virginia, touching the eastern edge of Kentucky before dipping down through the center of Tennessee. Granddaddy's slave master, Mr. William Burrus, bought both my grandfather and my father, along with other Africans.

When slaves were freed, or what was called "manumitted," if they had not been given a name they were allowed to select their own. However, Mr. Burrus, for whatever reason, had a practice of naming all of his slaves after himself. So there are a lot of us Burrus' running around today.

Mr. Burrus was a proud member of the Ku Klux Klan. The Ku Klux Klan was a secret society formed in 1915 that used acts of terrorism to suppress the freed black slaves, to prevent them from being accepted in society, and to reassert white supremacy over them.

So, as odd as it may sound today, I am a black man who bears the name of a former high-level

member of the Ku Klux Klan. However, in addition to that, I bear the name of the Lord Jesus Christ— I'm a Christian.

Mr. William Burrus, my grandfather's slave master, had a twisted set of values. Although some slave owners were cruel task masters, it wasn't uncommon in those days to find slave owners who privately felt a certain fondness for their slaves—

particularly the older ones who had served them faithfully. Such was the case with Mr. Burrus. He would sometimes call my grandfather aside and say, "Bill we're gonna ride tonight." That's all he would say. But my grandfather knew what that meant. It was a sort of code which meant that the Klansmen were going to ride horseback, hooded with their faces covered to beat black people.

So later, when they arrived at my grandparent's house, and kicked the door open, asking my grandmother, "Where's your husband? Where's that nigger, Bill?" She would honestly reply, "Sir, I don't know." For having received the warning from his thoughtful owner, Granddaddy would climb up through the chimney and hide in the woods until the Klan had left.

He often said he felt a great relief to hear them say, "Well, we'll get him next time." Then they'd ride off to find another poor unsuspecting soul to beat senseless simply because he was black.

Dear reader, may I encourage you to never mock an *unchangeable* characteristic you see in another person regardless of their color? My grandparents lived like that for many years, during which time my father was born.

Daddy was a bright young man who worked hard at menial jobs. He graduated from high school, and eventually from Meharry Medical College (a Methodist School founded in 1876, which is located in Nashville, Tennessee). He earned a doctorate in medicine. To be a licensed black medical doctor was an enviable position in those days. But his prestigious position, for which he had worked so hard, was to be short lived.

A white family in the community persuaded Daddy to abort their unwed daughter's baby. When word got out that he had done that, his license was immediately revoked, his dreams dashed, and he would never be licensed to practice medicine again.

Sadly, as a physician, he had violated the Hippocratic Oath which he and all doctors take, which in part says: *"I will prescribe regimens for the good* of my patients according to my ability and my judgment and *never do harm* to anyone. I will give *no deadly medicine* to any one if asked, nor suggest any such counsel; and similarly I will not give a woman a pessary *to cause an abortion*. But I will preserve *the purity of my life and my arts*."

More importantly, Daddy violated one of God's laws when he provided the abortion. Dear reader, never compromise your faith. You see, we have an advantage over some in the past. God tells us that "to whom much is given, much shall be required." As long as we live, we will be constantly challenged to compromise our faith. God's prophet Isaiah was quite determined in this regard. He wrote in Isaiah 50:7, *"Because the Sovereign Lord helps me, I will not be disgraced. Therefore have I set my face like a flint, and I know I will not be put to shame."*

Daddy married Elizabeth Holdman and God blessed them with children—13 in all. There were Frank, Bob, Bill, Rosco, Richael, Wilmouth, Floyd and later others. I don't remember all of their names.

One day in 1920, after the death of his dear wife Elizabeth, Daddy loaded all of his children in a mule-drawn wagon and moved the family from the Tennessee mountain plantation to the wide open spaces of Oklahoma. It was an arduous journey of almost 800 miles!

Upon arrival in Boley, Oklahoma Daddy met 19-year-old Gustava Brady Bennett, who stole his heart. He visited Boley's *Evening Light Saints Church* where young Gustava attended Sunday School. It didn't take long for him to ask her father Bro. Bennett for permission to marry her.

Mr. Bennett (my grandpa) called Gustava into the house and told her, "Gustava, you marry this man. He will make you a good husband."

Gustava replied, "But Daddy, I don't love him. I'm in love with Little Joe McDuffey."

"Just forget about Little Joe," Grandpa said. "Marry Dr. Burrus."

"Yes Daddy," she relented. "I'll quit Little Joe and marry Dr. Burrus." Sure enough, she dutifully called Little Joe in and told him it was over, and then she married my Daddy.

Daddy and his young bride (my dear Mother, Gustava) made their home in the bustling metropolis of Castle, Oklahoma. I'm only kidding, of course. Castle's entire population consisted of the members of seven families, most of whom were black. We were either sharecroppers, or we picked cotton. Even today, as I write this, according to the census, the population of Castle is only 106 souls.

However, they did their part to raise the population. God blessed them with 14 children, which included Rose, Anthony (me), Eular, Betty, Dr. Porter B. Burrus II, Erelene, Bobby Earl, Betty Earl, Gwendolyn and Belinda, and others whose names I've sadly forgotten.

## Chapter Three
# THE DIRTY THIRTIES

It's hard for us to even imagine today, but the cost of a gallon of gasoline in 1934 was $.10 cents per gallon. The price of a loaf of bread was $.08 cents; and a pound of hamburger was only $.12 cents. On top of that, 1934 was one of the worst financial years of the Great Depression. By then, the world's economy had literally plummeted.

Our little village of Castle sat right in the middle of what was called "the Dust Bowl." The years we lived there were called the "Dirty Thirties." It was a period of ravaging drought, when summer temperatures reached 117 degrees Fahrenheit, and dust storms eventually eroded one hundred million acres of fertile farmland.

Our family barely survived. Tens of thousands of families abandoned their farms and moved to other states. Many of the "Okies," as they were called, migrated to California only to discover that the conditions in California during the depression weren't much better than those in Oklahoma.

Castle, as I mentioned earlier, consisted of a handful of small bungalows, set off in cotton fields. They weren't clustered together like one might think of a small town...not at all. Castle's houses were separated by a mile or more.

On Sundays, we would often go to the Camp Meeting Grounds at Boley, Oklahoma, where Daddy and Mother met. Boley had established itself as an all-black town near the turn of the twentieth century. In the 30's it had essentially remained a black town, run by blacks, with a black mayor, police chief, and a black banker. One of the town's signs touted, "Facts About Boley, Oklahoma. *The Largest and Wealthiest Exclusive Negro City in the World*." The famed Booker T. Washington described Boley as "the finest black town in the world." I was always fond of our family's weekend trips to Boley.

Our little two-room, wood-framed house in Castle wasn't much. We had a wood-burning stove in the kitchen and an ice box. What I remember most was that in one room, Daddy would store the cotton that we'd picked. We children would play and jump in it, and at night we'd sleep on it until it was sold and picked up.

Our mother cooked incredible fried chicken on her wood burning cast iron stove. She also cooked delicious chicken and dumplings, collard greens, cabbage, mustard greens and fried okra fresh from our family garden.

Cooking fried chicken back then wasn't as simple as it is today. Our family's chickens were free range, or cage free chickens. Of course we fed them, but they also lived off the environment as they wandered freely throughout the yard.

So, on a day when Mother was going to prepare chicken, which was normally on a Sunday after church, she'd go to the back porch and take her "catching wire" that hung on a nail. It looked like a straightened out wire coat hanger with a crook formed on one end.

Then Mother would step into the yard and corral a hand full of chickens in a corner of the yard and slip that wire underneath one of them and grab it by the leg. By then, it was all over. I guess chickens must have poor eyesight. They never seemed to see that wire comin'.

As she pulled that snared chicken toward her it would squawk and flail about wildly for a moment. But she would calmly grasp its head in her hand, and with a quick flick of her wrist, she'd ring its neck--that is what we called it.

As a young boy, I remember how puzzling it was to see those headless chickens run wildly back and forth across the yard before they fell over. Daddy explained that the chicken was actually dead. Those were simply its nerve and muscle responses. But it fascinated me nonetheless.

Next, Mother would take the chicken inside where she had a large pot of boiling water. She'd clean it, then dip it in scalding water, and pluck its feathers. Sometimes I got to help. Once featherless, she'd wash the chicken, cut it into pieces, dip each piece in her special batter and drop it in the crackling hot grease.

The Kentucky Colonel had nothing on my mother. Of course, he had yet to discover his seven secret spices, but it couldn't have come close to my mother's recipe. By the time that chicken was getting golden brown, Mother was mashing potatoes, and pulling her homemade biscuits out of the oven.

The house smelled heavenly! Sometimes I can almost recapture that fragrance. A little cream gravy, and it wasn't hard to get anyone to the table around the Burrus' house. However, with all of the children in our family, we ate in shifts.

## Chapter Four
# TROUBLESOME TIMES

**B**ack in Tennessee, Mr. Burrus, our family's slave master had divided some of his property and given it to his slaves. Even then, the hand of God was over my family. My father, through my grandfather, inherited some of that wealth. However, when you inherit wealth quickly, if you don't know its value and how to be a steward of it, it will destroy you.

So it was with Daddy. He made some hasty decisions regarding his children. *First, he decided that his children would never know hunger* as he had known hunger. That was his first mistake. *Second, he determined that he would never allow his children to suffer.* Although our father meant well, he didn't know that destitution and suffering are sometimes part of the process, the training grounds, through which God develops and strengthens us.

So with that in mind, my father bought Bob and Bill, two of my older brothers a new car every year. Back then cars cost about $400 dollars each. Then my ungrateful and undisciplined brothers would speed, get ticketed or worse—get arrested.

Attempting to be a good father, Daddy would bail them out of jail. Looking back on it now, I don't think they ever spent a full day behind bars, which was exactly what they needed. Instead, he bailed them out time and time again. Eventually, they broke him. Unfortunately, as adults, Bob and Bill later became professional thieves. They would steal anything that wasn't nailed down; then when asked about it, they'd lie.

So by the time we younger siblings were born, Daddy had learned how to rear children, *and impressed upon us the value of hard work.*

We didn't know until after Daddy was released from McAllister State Prison that he'd been incarcerated for refusing to expose my brothers, Bob and Bill, who likely stole the molasses from Johnson's farm. He took their punishment. It's reminiscent of what our Lord Jesus did for us, isn't it? We were the guilty sinners, yet He paid the price for our sin. The innocent became guilty, so the guilty could go free!

To Daddy's credit, as long as he lived, he never mentioned the fact that it was my testimony, as a five-year-old child, that sent him to prison. He loved me so much that he never wanted me to feel responsible for his imprisonment.

My experience at age five was a pivotal point in my life. At five years of age I learned to *stay away from white people; not to ever get close to them; and never to trust them. They'll take your Daddy away and lock him up in the penitentiary.* With that merciless act, seeds of hatred were planted in my little heart. Prior to that, I had never hated anyone. Two fellow human beings misused their authority and taught me to hate. *Dear reader, don't ever abuse or mistreat a child. What we plant in the heart of a child remains, and grows. Sometimes it redirects a person for a lifetime.*

As I grew older, that fear became dislike, and the dislike turned into hatred. Hatred drove me to the brink of becoming a black revolutionary. As a teen we'd walk through the streets singing, "Sing it loud: I'm black and I'm proud. Sing it loud: I'm black and I'm proud. Sing it loud: I'm black and I'm proud." In my youth that sounded good, but now as an adult, I realize how stupid it was. God hates pride.

But as a child when I was living through it, I felt threatened by white folks. In my heart I determined to stay away from those people. I was afraid to even say hello to them because I lived with an irrational fear that said, *they will take your Daddy away from you.* Fear is monstrous. It's debilitating.

## Chapter Five
# HARDSHIP

The year Daddy was in prison was extremely tough for our family. We hadn't really appreciated him, or realized how dependent we were upon him until we were left to fend for ourselves. We would later learn that it wasn't easy for him either. The State Prison, built in 1909, was designed after the federal prison at Fort Leavenworth, Kansas. Daddy had been sorely ill-treated while in prison.

One late fall day in 1935, we children were playing outside when we spotted a man walking across the cotton field toward our house. Suddenly, Mother dried her hands on her apron, ran outside and shouted at the top of her lungs, "Children, your Daddy's home, your Daddy's home!"

My younger brother, who had been born while he was away, had no idea who he was. But as you can guess, they quickly became friends. Daddy always loved his children. Like I mentioned earlier, even today as I look back, I'm touched by the fact that he never held my confession that sent him to prison against me. Daddy never mentioned it, not wanting me to ever feel responsible. Instead, he lived a righteous life and taught us, "Children, you don't ever want to go to jail. Jail is for bad, bad people."

Upon his release, since he could no longer practice medicine, Daddy developed his own small truck-patching business. Unfamiliar with truck-patching, are you? Well, a truck-patch was a relatively small family garden in which one produced fruit and vegetables to be sold door-to-door.

My family tended two vegetable gardens. One was to feed our family, and the other provided fruit and vegetables for Daddy to sell. We children shared the responsibility of tilling the soil, pulling the weeds, and helping with the harvest. Both gardens contained collard greens, turnip greens, corn, spinach, beans, onions, okra and more. To support the family, we would help Daddy harvest the food from our truck-patch, and he would peddle it to the other families out of a sack on his back. I suppose we could say that he was an early entrepreneur--a street vendor.

Mother had no time to work outside the home. As was the case with most of the women of her era, she was a fulltime work-at-home Mother. Remember, between her and Daddy, I had 25 siblings, of which I was number 14! When Mother married my widowed Daddy, he already had 13 children, and as strange as it seems, his oldest son was only four years younger than her. However, once they were wed, all of the children grew to love her. Loving and caring for them was her life's work.

We were poor, so poor that the poor people called us poor! But we were rich in relationships. When I was in the second grade I had no school clothes to wear, so I wore my sister Rose's dresses. Mother would make simple dresses for Rose and me to wear from the food sacks we received from the government. "Contains government food, not to be resold," was even printed on the sacks. When company came by the house, I'd hide from embarrassment.

Because I had skipped the second grade for lack of clothes to wear, the next year when I entered the second grade I was already the size of a third grader--bigger than all of the other boys in my class.

Due to my size, the football coach recruited me for the team. During one of the first games of the season, he insisted that I carry the ball, because I was the biggest. Somewhere, even at that young age, I had picked up the mistaken idea that if you're big, you can run over people.

So, when the ball was snapped and handed to me, I ran full speed toward that line of little bitty boys. Suddenly one of them hit me around the ankles, turned me a complete flip, and knocked the breath out of me. When I stopped seeing stars, I realized that my football career had ended before it began. I never played football again. No way.

I've told you how we grew our own vegetables and raised our own chickens from which we got both eggs and meat. We'd also hunt and kill rabbits, opossums, and squirrels to eat. When the neighbors would butcher a hog, they'd generously share some of their fresh pork with us as well.

We Burrus' always celebrated Christmas a day later than the other families in Castle. The day after Christmas, on December 26th, my father and I would wake up early, get dressed, and take two gunny sacks out the door. We would walk one and a half miles to town where we would go through the alleys behind the houses of the rich folk. To us they were rich, because they made as much as a whopping $2.00 per hour!

We would dig through their garbage cans searching for turkey carcasses, partially eaten apples and oranges, pastries, and pieces of discarded candy. Then later at home, after Mother cleaned it, she'd serve it and we'd sit down at the table, bow our heads and thank God for providing for our needs. To us, that was Christmas.

The neighbor kids would say, "Your daddy lives out of the garbage cans." Being a child I thought as a child, so I would deny it. I'd reply, "Oh, we're rich. We don't... Who would do that?" The reason I can share that with you now is because God has emancipated me. I'm a free man! I'm free from the slavery, the power, and the consequences of sin! *I'm free from the opinions of others as well.*

We black children weren't allowed to attend the white schools. We often wondered why, and what happened over there in the white school. Once a year, city school superintendent, Mr. Christianson, would drop by our black school to encourage us. He would tell us, "You boys are great. We expect you to grow up big and strong. You're going to be the greatest farmers in the world. You'll feed this great nation of ours. Without fellows like you, America would fall. You can plant rows of cotton and corn that are as straight as an arrow." That was the highest dream that we dared to dream.

Every time I heard him say that, my little chest would pop out with pride, as did those of my schoolmates. We thought, "Man, we're important. America needs us." So everything we did, we did our best. We graded and picked cotton the best we could. We wanted to be the best farmers in the world.

However, across the tracks at the school for the white kids, he'd tell them, "You youngsters will become our doctors, lawyers, the professors and leaders; and perhaps even a president of this great nation of ours. You need to study hard and make good grades so you can graduate and enroll in college." They were allowed to dream of becoming college-trained professionals. But not us, we were black.

## Chapter Six

# LIFE IN WEWOKA

At 10-years-old we had moved from Castle to Wewoka, Oklahoma—the capitol of the Seminole Nation. To us, Wewoka was a metropolis. You see, in 1925 oil was discovered one and a half miles southeast of Wewoka. So by the mid-thirties unprecedented barrels of oil were flowing and the population had grown to more than 20,000 people. It was the third-largest city in Oklahoma! If you and your family lived in Wewoka, you were successful!

Wewoka even had streets and avenues with numbers and *names on them*! There was First Street, Second Street, Ocheese Avenue, Eufaula Avenue, Hitchite Avenue and Okfuskee Avenue.

As we moved the 26 miles from Castle to Wewoka we felt like someone must have felt moving from Myrtle, Mississippi to New York City! Today, however, the population of Wewoka is a little more than 3,500.

I made friends quickly in Wewoka. One night, three friends and I were walking down the street past a neighborhood church that was in revival.

Those revived saints were singing at the top of their lungs. We had no air conditioning, so the church windows were wide open and the sound carried for blocks! I might add delicately that the singing left something to be desired.

I turned to one of my buddies and said, "Them folks sound like a bunch of billy goats." We laughed. Then one of my friends said, "I bet you won't go in there and tell them folks that they sound like a bunch of billy goats." (Here's a word of caution. Never dare a fool to do anything.)

"Certainly, I will," I boldly said.

"Then let's go," he replied and we turned and traipsed up the steps, through the front door and into that noisy auditorium. Half scared to death; we sat down on the first available row of seats, near the back.

When the music ended the pastor stood and welcomed the people. Then he said, "I feel like there is someone in here who has a word of testimony to share with the congregation." He paused momentarily to allow someone to speak. My friends all turned and looked at me and whispered, "Go ahead. Go down there. You said you'd tell these folks they sound like a bunch of billy goats."

I was petrified with fear. I was trapped. I was scared to death, but also afraid to lose street credibility with my buddies. I lifted my hand slowly and the pastor saw it immediately.

"Yes, young man," he said. "Come on down here and share a word from the Lord with us."

My buddies showed me no mercy. They prodded and pushed until I stood and stumbled out into the aisle. I'm still not sure how I made it from the back of the church to the front, but I did.

"Go ahead young man," the pastor urged.

"Yes sir! You preach it...share what's on your heart," the congregation began to shout.

"Uh...," I struggled to mouth the words. It was too late to turn back. My bragging and boastful attitude had gotten me in this predicament.

From the back I could see my friends trying to hold back their laughter. One was mouthing the words, "You said you would tell them."

"I just came to tell you folks that your singing sounds like a bunch of billy goats." I vaguely remember their gasps and the shocked look on their faces, but that is all. Immediately two giant invisible hands picked me up and slammed me down on the floor in front of them. Those two hands wrestled and shook me violently under the front benches. In the process a remarkable and eternal transformation took place. I was changed--a totally new creation in Christ.

Of course I couldn't have described to you what had happened; but when I stood moments later, I wasn't the same boy.

One of the parishioners asked if I was alright. I assured him I was. Then to explain myself I said, "I think I just became one of you billy goats." With that, they all began to praise God.

Afterward I ran straight home, walked into our little house and told Mother what I'd experienced; and what I had told the church. She embraced me and told me how very proud she was of me. That was the night I experienced the new birth. I was eternally saved as Christ Jesus came to live in my heart.

Daddy continued to sharecrop and truck-patch. We continued to grow fruit and vegetables, raise chickens, and gather eggs to sell to the neighbors. He would carry them on his back as he walked his route.

Perhaps because he had lost his medical license and his career, Daddy was obsessed with the notion that every one of his children would become doctors. That obsession, sad to say, made me hate him. All the other children in the neighborhood could play outside, but we couldn't. "Sit down," he'd demand. "You've got to learn to trace a drop of blood through every part of the body." We did. We learned about the right tricuspid and the left tricuspid heart valves. But who wanted to know about that?

I knew that I couldn't defy him or he'd beat me to death. I resigned myself to the fact I would sit there and learn everything that Daddy was teaching us. But I knew when I became 18-years-old I was going to forget it all. So I sat there and learned it, knowing all along that it was foolishness.

As I learned it, I made an important discovery. I learned that one can't forget what he learns. What we learn is forever imprinted in our brains. Or as the late Oliver Wendell Holmes, Jr. put it, "A mind that is stretched by a new experience can never go back to its old dimensions." In my mid-80s today, I still use what Daddy taught us about medicine and the human body virtually every day.

In spite of what my Daddy taught me, I still did not believe I possessed the ability to learn. Because of this, I stumbled through high school, barely graduating with a C average.

To their credit, perhaps as a result of their experiences with Bob and Bill, our parents sheltered us. We weren't allowed to go out and experience life. So our life in Wewoka was stable.

## Chapter Seven
# "GO WEST, YOUNG MAN..."

In the mid 40's, my parents heard that California was a non-segregated, integrated state. We could hardly imagine such a place, but began the process of moving out there. Daddy and my older brothers, Bill and Bob went first. They arrived in Richmond, California, across the bay from San Francisco; where before long, Bill opened a nightclub and restaurant on Grove Street in North Richmond.

This was the era of the Brown Derby, so he named his nightclub "The Brown Derby." Before long, it became the biggest nightclub in Richmond and the center for gambling in the area. I didn't have a problem with gambling at the time. I loved my big brother. After all, nobody was getting beat up, so I saw nothing wrong with it.

In 1947, once Daddy got settled, he returned for the family. Our entire family piled into a '46 Buick and a '46 Ford and left the racially segregated State of Oklahoma for the supposedly integrated state of California, thinking we would free

41

ourselves from segregation. We quickly learned that wasn't to be the case. It was different, however.

As Oklahoma sharecroppers who helped raise the landowner's crops, we shared the crops we raised. We were told, "You can live here free. All you have to do is tend this land and grow these crops. When you need groceries, go to the store and get them. If you don't have the money at that time, just sign the ticket and get them on credit. At the end of the year we will settle up and you can pay whatever you owe me then." Although it was a hard life, we understood it. Life in California was to be quite different.

Our realtors, Jack and Rena Pryde, promised to help us. They sold us our California home at 1318 Filbert Street in North Richmond. It was a whole new world for me.

Unlike Oklahoma, in California we saw no signs saying "Colored Only," or "Whites Only," but our neighbors were different. They were Spanish speaking. In fact, we were surrounded by Mexicans, Italians, Portuguese, Chinese, Filipinos, and Laotians. There were NO white people in our neighborhood.

We would later learn that Richmond was a "red-lined city." Mr. and Mrs. Pryde were, as were other realtors, in cahoots with the bankers. When we went to the bank we were not allowed past the front desk because we were black. You see, on the wall in the back office where transactions were typically negotiated and contracts were signed, was a large city map. On that map, certain sections of the city were encircled with red lines. Realtors and bank personnel were instructed not to sell property to African-Americans, and other minorities outside of the red line. "Red-lining," as it was called, was to keep non-whites confined to the same neighborhoods.

Richmond's red lines were between two sets of railroad tracks, just below a manufacturing plant which continuously poured pollutants into the air. We were steered away from property in the hills, where the air was clean. Bankers wouldn't approve loans for colored folks to buy property outside of that polluted red circle.

Our home at 1318 Filbert Street had a big Weeping Willow tree in the back yard. The neighborhood children and I loved climbing in that big tree. My dear friend Rudy often played and ate at my house; then he'd invite me to his house to play and eat. Rudy taught me to cook Mexican chili verde con tortillas de maiz. It was really, really good.

When the Laotian families began moving into our neighborhood, we did the same cultural exchange. Their food was quite different. Steamed

43

sticky rice with chicken and green leaves called Pax Som. Pax Som was the equivalent of Mexican Habanero peppers, which are one hundred times hotter than Jalapenos. We learned the hard way. Stay away from Pax Som!

With people come their languages. I learned to eat like Mexicans, speak like Mexicans and my friends referred to me as "The Black Mexican," or "The King of Spanish." I also learned to converse in Italian, Lao, Spanish, and Tagalog (the language Filipinos speak). I preach in Laotian.

Mother enrolled me in Richmond Union High School, which though integrated, was only physically integrated. But as I've said, I was thoroughly convinced that I was inferior. Today, as an educator looking back at it, I can clearly see that the system had been deliberately designed to teach me, and those like me, that we were inferior. And it was made clear to us that we could never go to college, for we would never be bright enough to graduate.

As I sat in class and listened to my German teacher teach in English, his English sounded to me like a foreign language. I couldn't understand what on earth he was saying, and I didn't dare raise my hand and ask, because I'd reveal how little I knew, and I didn't want to be considered dumb. So I faked and bluffed my way through.

At that time, my two biggest fears were rattlesnakes and beautiful girls. Both of which scared me to death.

On the day of my senior prom, Mother promised to buy me a new suit if I would go. I said, "Well, Mother, you can keep your suit, 'cause I'm not going." The reason I didn't want to go was because my schoolmates had teased and threatened me. They said if I attended the prom, they'd make me dance with Lily Mae Wynn, who was the prettiest girl in the whole city. I was so scared that I ran a mile and a half home from school that day.

In June of 1948 I graduated from high school with my body integrated, but my mind still quite segregated. I barely graduated with a "C" grade average in my graduating class of 645 students.

Most of us black students didn't leave for college upon graduation. Instead, we became common laborers who dug ditches, mowed lawns, washed windows, etc. We did whatever we could to earn money.

One day in 1949, while sitting under the big Willow tree in our backyard I received a revelation. I was tired of being broke and begging. So I gathered the neighborhood kids under that big tree and began teaching them Spanish for ten cents a lesson. I wasn't that good at math, but I quickly figured that if I could get five kids at that rate, I'd make fifty cents an hour. And if I could enroll 10 kids, that would be one whole U.S. dollar! You talk about somebody working, I immediately began teaching 10 students under that tree, and before long I was making up to $2.00 dollars an hour. That meant mega bucks to me!

I enjoyed teaching children under that tree. Some of my students later went away to college, and a couple actually became teachers themselves. Some would ask me, "Why don't you enroll in college, Anthony?"

Unwilling to admit the truth, I'd say, "Why? Look at me. I'm making mega bucks here. I don't need to go to college."

However, the truth was I was secretly convinced that people of color would never thrive in college. College was for white folks.

## Chapter Eight
# GIVING IT THE OLD COLLEGE TRY

I finally broke down and enrolled in the two-year program at Contra Costa Community College in 1952. But I flunked out after one semester with all "F's" in English. I received a letter from the college that read, "Mr. Burrus, please find another institution of higher learning. Your grades are an embarrassment to us."

I wrote back, "Please, if you would just allow me to come back to college on probation, I promise I will do better." Honestly, I felt that I was really doing the best I could.

They replied, "Very well. You can return on probation, but if your grades don't improve, you'll be expelled permanently."

So, in 1953, at the age of 23, I decided to give college another try. As I walked down the hall I saw a sign on a classroom door that read, "Anthropology." I had no idea what that was, but it was a big impressive word, and I liked that. So I enrolled in the class. To my surprise, I actually enjoyed it.

Then I saw another sign that said, "Sociology." So I took that one too, and I enjoyed it also. In fact, I made straight A's! I thought, *man, college is fun. Who told me that I would never do well in college?*

Next I took "Psychology," and again I made straights A's! I didn't have sense enough to mix some easy subjects along with the harder ones. I took all of the subjects that I liked. In doing so, I learned that I could not only learn, but that learning was fun. Then I thought *who did this to me? Who said I was inferior? Who told me that I couldn't learn?*

I enrolled in a Spanish 101. The first morning the instructor welcomed us to class saying, "Who can tell us how to say 'good morning' in Spanish?"

I threw my hand straight up excitedly and began to wave. I knew it. I had taught my children that in my backyard classes under the Willow tree back home.

He apparently suspected that I, the black ghetto kid, wouldn't know Spanish, so he kept asking. "Someone tell me how do you say 'Good morning' in Spanish."

I was all but jumping out of my chair, when he finally broke down and asked me, "Alright, young man, how do you say 'good morning' in Spanish?"

"Buenos Dias," I blurted out in pure Spanish.

He was shocked, and continued. "Then who can tell me how to say 'what time is it?'"

"Que hora es?" I responded loudly.

I kept answering questions so quickly, clearly, and correctly that he finally made his way over to my chair and said quietly, "Señor, if you will just be quiet I will give you an A for the whole semester."

Since I already knew what my semester grade was going to be, Spanish class was "free time" for me. To make full use of it, I went to the school library and checked out an Italian language textbook, and while the rest of the class learned Spanish, I taught myself Italian—in my Spanish class!

When the next semester rolled around I enrolled in Italian 101, and there too I was seated on the front row when the professor walked in and said, "Good morning students. Who can tell me how to say 'good morning' in Italian?" You guessed it.

I said with gusto, "Buongiorno!"

"Okay, sir. How do you say, 'I'm hungry, let's go eat?' in Italian.

"Ho fame. Andiamo a mangiare." I said with a smile.

"That's correct. Sir, if you will just be quiet I will give you an A for the whole semester."

So while my fellow students learned Italian, I checked a French language book out of the school library and taught myself French.

Of course, in my next semester I was met with, "How do you say "good morning" in French?" And of course, the same thing occurred.

It was also 1952 when I awoke one morning having had a vision of sheep without a shepherd. I shared my experience with my parents telling them, "God is calling me into the ministry." They encouraged me to get the counsel of our pastor, which I did.

With their encouragement, I walked the aisle of our church one Sunday and announced to the congregation God's call upon my life. They rejoiced with the news and I was invited to preach my first sermon.

They licensed me to preach and ordained me to the ministry. Over the following years I pastored churches in Richmond, Oakland, and Hayward, California.

School however was a different story. Years before I had grown weary of people calling me "dumb," "boy," and "nigger." I was tired of people saying things like "Boy, get out of here. We hate you." I knew I had to do something about it.

Clearly I couldn't change other people, or fight everyone who called me a bad name. Instead, I got on my knees and prayed, *"God, please give me an ability that I can do so well that I will earn the respect of other men."*

God didn't say, "Okay." Instead, He gave me a remarkable discovery: learn. Learning languages came easy to me. In 1956, at 27 years of age, I graduated from Contra Costa College with five financial scholarships and a trophy. The trophy bore a plaque that read, "King of Spanish."

## Chapter Nine
# A LOVE STORY

As a boy I was often laughed at, and made fun of. Friends called me tall, lanky, ugly, and worse. They convinced me that I was ugly. Plus, remember, I was terrified of snakes and pretty girls. I could never ever strike up a conversation with a girl.

In 1967, when I was 38-years-old, Sister Matty Trailer, my mother's friend from church, told my mother about her 29-year-old unmarried cousin, and said, "You just tell your Anthony to call this number."

That telephone number belonged to Alex Fisher, the uncle of Billie Faye Fisher who later became my wife.

I had injured my back while driving for the public transportation company and wound up in the hospital. Mother came for a visit and when she walked into my room, she handed me the phone number. She said, "Brother, (she always called me Brother) Sister Trailer said for you to call this number."

Obediently I replied, "Yes, Mother. I'll call it."

The next day, here came Mother again. "Good morning, Brother. How are you feeling today?"

"I'm doing all right, Mother."

"Did you call the phone number I gave you, like you promised?"

"No, Mother, but I'm going to make the call today."

Then I got one of those looks from her, and the message was loud and clear. *There's only one way to get your Mother off your back and that's to do what she's said and call that number.*

So, later that day I dialed that number and it rang once. I was thinking, *please don't answer. Please don't answer.* Nobody answered. I said, "Great, nobody's home."

It rang a second time. Again, no one answered. I said, "Hallelujah! I'm home free."

But when the phone rang the third time, someone with a soft feminine voice said, "Hello?"

Shocked, and off guard, I caught myself saying, "Oh Lord…"

The voice on the other end of the line said, "Who is this? What did you say?"

I stuttered, "Uh, I'm Anthony, Anthony Burrus." I would have usually said, "I'm the Reverend Anthony Burrus." Looking back on it now, perhaps it's good that I didn't, because at the time I didn't know that Billie Faye had often said she would never marry a preacher.

She asked, "What do you want?"

I explained nervously, "My mother told me that her friend Mrs. Trailer said I should call you, so I'm calling you now."

Then for whatever odd reason, I asked, "Are you beautiful?"

She replied quizzically, "No."

I found it hard to believe her, because I wondered, *why would my Mother hook me up with an ugly girl?*

She said, "No, I'm not beautiful."

"Are you fun to be with?"

She answered, "No. Not particularly."

Oh, man. I thought, *why in the world would Mother hook me up with an ugly girl who's no fun?*

So, we talked and I finally worked up enough courage to say, "Billie Faye, if ever you're ever in my fair city, call me. I'd like to meet you."

Of course I assumed *she'll never, ever come back to this town--never again.*

However, two weeks later her cousin passed away, and I was asked to help conduct the funeral.

Remember, all I knew about her was that she was homely-looking and no fun at all. So, I was standing at the pulpit when halfway through the funeral I saw a man and a glorious looking young lady come through the door—late. In fact they were about 40 minutes late for the funeral!

I had no idea who they were, but thought to myself, "That's certainly an attractive young lady." But of course from the pulpit I didn't say anything.

When the service concluded and it was time to view the body, everyone stood and walked past the casket. Then the casket was taken outside to the hearse and driven to the burial site.

We ministers marched along behind the casket, and as the casket march passed her aisle, I just had to take a peek. "Whoa!" I thought. "Whoever she is, she is beautiful!"

Then I exited the building and we proceeded to the cemetery for the interment. Once done, I returned home and swallowed a handful of pain pills because my back was killing me. I had barely crawled into bed when the phone rang.

"Hello?" I said.

"Anthony, you said if I was ever in your fair city, to call you. Well, I'm in your fair city and I'm calling you. You promised that if I'd call, you'd come over to meet me."

I said, "Where are you?"

"I'm staying at 1428 Third Street."

"I'll be there in 75 seconds."

Those were my exact words. I sprang out of bed, got dressed, put on my clerical (backward) collar, jumped into my car and drove across town.

As I pulled up in front of the house, I was amazed. The yard was clean. There was not one piece of trash; no dogs or chickens were running around. The blinds and drapes were closed. However, the house was surrounded by cars.

I walked up to the door and rang the doorbell. "Come in." I heard.

Slowly and cautiously I opened the door and stepped inside. There was a crowd of people crammed into that little house. I learned that they were relatives who had gathered to comfort and support the family of the deceased. But sitting beside the door, was the stunning young lady I'd seen earlier at the funeral. I looked at her and I thought, "A girl that pretty would never speak to me." I ignored her out of fear.

I continued to the back of the house into the kitchen, looking for the ugly girl I'd talked with on the phone. Once there, an older lady put her hand on my shoulder, turned me around, and said, "Let me take you up front. I want you to meet Billie Faye." With that, she walked me right back to the front door.

And this devastatingly attractive lady I'd seen when I walked in smiled and said, "Hi, I'm Billie."

I stammered apprehensively, "I'm Anthony." I could feel all those church folk staring at me, the reverend, with my backward collar on. So, out of fear, there was only one sensible thing for me to do. Can you guess what I did? *I ran.* I ran to the front door.

Billie decided that there was only one thing for her to do. She ran after me. In fact, we tried to run through the front door at the same time and got stuck! I threw my hands up in surrender and said, "I'm scared."

She said, "You're scared? *I'm the one who's scared.*"

"What?" I said, "What could you possibly be afraid of?

She said, *"Of you,* of course."

It was funny, once we'd both admitted our fear, we could relate.

We made it down about five steps on the porch when I said, *"I'm going to marry you, Billie Faye."*

Never had I ever even asked a girl out—never in my life!

She replied, "Anthony, I already have a boyfriend."

I said, "Billie Faye Fisher, that doesn't matter. I'm going to marry you." Then I asked, "Are you headed home now?"

She said, "Yes. I have to go home, Anthony."

"Well, my house is on the way to your house, so why don't I take you home?"

"Okay," she conceded.

By the time we arrived at her house in San Jose my back was killing me. I could hardly stand the pain. So I pointed out the window to distract her and said, "Look at that beautiful tree."

As she turned to look, I managed to pull my aching back out of the car, and hobble around to her side. I didn't want her to know that I could barely stand at this point. I was literally leaning on the side of the car in agony as I opened the door for her. As she climbed out and began walking up to the front door, I said, "Well, okay. I'll see you."

"Alright," she agreed.

I drove about two blocks then pulled over to the curb, turned off the engine, and fell asleep.

Several hours later I awoke and drove back home. Over the next few weeks we continued talking and finally, I worked up the courage to really ask her to marry me.

## Chapter Ten
# NEWLY WED

August 20th, 1967 was a beautiful day. That was the day that Billie Faye Fisher became Mrs. Anthony Burrus as we were wed in Highbank, Texas, southeast of the beautiful central Texas town of Waco. We had a lovely wedding and a joyful celebration.

My brother-in-law thoughtfully arranged for us to drive his daddy's car on our honeymoon. The only problem was that after the wedding he returned to Cisco, Texas with the car keys in his pocket! So, there we were, newly wed, and stuck out there in that little country church in the middle of a cotton field, in the dark with no car keys.

This was long before cell phones. And that far out in the country one might even have trouble getting a cell phone signal today! So, we walked together down the road to a farmhouse, knocked on the door and asked if we could call Billie Faye's daddy and tell him we were stuck.

Mr. Fisher graciously came to our rescue and we spent our entire honeymoon at my mother- and father-in-law's house in Marlin, Texas. It was awkward to say the least. Don't get me wrong, Marlin was, and I'm sure it still is a nice place, but it was no vacation paradise.

After our rather unorthodox honeymoon, we returned to Berkley, California where we set up housekeeping in my sister's rent house at 1520 Sacramento Street. God gave us three wonderful children. Our eldest is our daughter, Enda; our son, Enzi; and finally our baby daughter, Heri.

I remember one day during that time, Billie Faye asked, "Anthony, can I get a job to help pay our bills?"

I said, "No Dear, it's too expensive for you to work. You just stay home and raise our children. I'll work." So she did.

In 1999, my beautiful wife and I along with our three children, moved from California to Hewitt, Texas, outside of Waco. Some may find this hard to believe, but in 39 years and six months of marriage, Billie Faye and I never had one serious argument. Ours was a wonderful marriage.

Then the next year, the unthinkable happened. In 2000, dear Billie Faye was diagnosed with Multiple Myeloma—cancer of the blood. I was forced to retire from teaching to care for her and our three children. She would complain of pain while lying on her back. But when I turned her on her right side, she would shout, "Ouch! Turn me on my left side." When I did she would again yell in pain, "Help me get on my back." Then once on her back, she'd cringe again.

The only relief she found was when she rode in our car. So to provide her with much needed relief I would drive to Dallas, turn around and ride back to Waco. The round trip took about three hours during which she could sleep with the car moving. We sometimes drove all day, back and forth from Waco to Dallas. As the sun would set she would cry and beg me for just one more trip to Dallas. We were both so weary. There were many days when she would sit in her wheel chair and just weep from the intense pain.

One day as we were leaving the medical clinic following her checkup, we stopped at the cashier's window. The office assistance rang up the total, which was $200 dollars. As I reached for my checkbook she smiled and said, "Mr. Burrus, your bill has been paid in full. You owe nothing."

Billie Faye went home to be with the Lord in 2001, leaving a hospital bill of $16,000 dollars. Shortly after her death, the phone rang and a man on the other end of the line said, "I understand you recently lost your wife."

I said, "Yes, sir."

"Tell me how much your bill is," he said.

"$16,000 dollars," I replied.

He rather abruptly hung up.

One week later I received a letter from the hospital thanking me for paying our bill so promptly. To this day I have no idea whose voice that was on the phone. I just thank Jesus.

## Chapter Eleven
# A SECOND BLESSING

After losing my dear wife, I decided to leave Texas and return to California. One day my daughter Heri called me. She told me that she had a young single lady sitting in her beauty shop in Waco that I should meet. I could hear in the tone of her voice what she was implying.

I said emphatically, "Daughter, NO WAY, NO HOW, NO! I am not interested. I am never ever gonna marry again—never, never, never."

Then I overheard Heri say to her customer, "Miss. Lula, I really want you to meet Daddy."

I couldn't help but smile when I heard Miss Lula reply, "Heri, if it's a man you want me to meet, NO WAY! I'm not looking for a man. I am never going to marry again—never, never, never."

Before I hung up, Heri made me write down Miss Lula's phone number. I suppose it was out of curiosity more than anything I called her.

We immediately connected. It felt like Lula and I had known each other all our lives. I asked her if she would like to fly out to California to meet my Mother and me. She said she would, so I sent her an airline ticket.

When Lula arrived, Mother put me out of the house saying, "Son, you'll need to find yourself another place to sleep for a few days while Miss Lula and I bond." At 100 years of age, she was still intent on looking out for her son. Three days after Miss Lula and I met face-to-face, we were engaged to be married.

In 2001, at the age of 101 years and six months, my sweet Mother took her flight from earth into the arms of Jesus.

Lula and I are still in love after all these years.

Anthony and Lula Burrus

In 1998, my mother made international news when at 98 years of age she realized her life-long dream of graduating from elementary, junior high, and high school. Interestingly, she graduated from the same high school I had graduated from in June of 1948!

Mr. Christopher Columbus Cousin handed my 98 year old Mother her diplomas that certified her three levels of education. Then Native American Apache Chief Chochise's granddaughter presented her with a gold plated letter opener. She was interviewed on a Tokyo, Japan television network, along with several American networks.

Ever the humorist Mother left her undergraduates with this warning, *"If you don't want to get old, oily, wrinkled and ugly—die young!"*

## Chapter Twelve
# LIFE LESSONS

Return with me to the 1950s. After graduating from Contra Costa College in 1956 I worked for one year; then in 1957 enrolled as a student in San Francisco State University with a major in Spanish, and a minor in Public Speaking. I noticed on a school bulletin board an advertisement that read, "We need a person who can speak Spanish to do some home tutoring in the Merced Apartments." I had no way of knowing that no black person had ever set foot in those apartments. All I knew was that the San Francisco State Spanish Department had approved me as a Spanish teacher, so I walked up to the apartment and rang the doorbell.

A teenager opened the door, and I said, "Hello, I'm Anthony Burrus. Someone here advertised at the university for a Spanish language private tutor. I'm here to fulfill that request. I'm a certified Spanish teacher."

The young man answered, "Oh, well, come on in. I'm the one who needs help with Spanish." We sat down, began to talk, and bonded almost immediately.

As he began to relax and open up, I began to teach him Spanish.

After about 30 minutes, the doorbell rang and he said, "That must be my mom."

His Mother walked in and saw me, a black man sitting at the table talking with her son, and didn't know quite what to think. He said, "Mom, this is my Spanish teacher, Mr. Burrus."

She said, "Oh, okay. What are your fees?" They were around $15 an hour as I recall.

I said, "Ma'am, the fee is $15 per hour, and I started half an hour ago."

She said, "Here's your pay for three hours. You can go now. Thank you." She paid me for three hours of teaching that I hadn't done then ushered me out the door!

On my way home I figured it out. She had paid to get rid of me because I was black. I ran into things like that continually in *integrated* California.

I was a student teacher, teaching Spanish at San Francisco's Luther Burbank Middle School when one day, I noticed a gentleman seated in the back of my classroom. I thought he might be the father of one of my students, but later learned he wasn't. He was a school principal who had heard about my teaching ability, and was there to observe me. Not knowing he was "scouting me," I lost track of my teaching outline or text book, and got caught up in teaching extemporaneously from my heart. The kids were all engaged, and so transfixed that when the bell rang they all gave a corporate sigh disappointment that class had ended.

As the students filed out of the classroom to their next classes, the man who had been sitting in my class approached me saying, "Hello, Mr. Burrus. My name is Dr. George Marr. I'm the principal at Emeryville Middle School, not far from here. We have some job openings for teachers, so I am here today to offer you an opportunity to teach at our school." I couldn't believe my ears. I was elated!

He was there to offer me a junior high school teaching position using provisional credentials, and they would pay me $7,500 per year! All I had to do was drop out of school and join them.

I literally ran to my education professor Dr. Marvin Silverman, a tall Jewish man who always held a pipe in his teeth.

"Dr. Silverman, Dr. Silverman..." I said breathlessly. "I'm finally dropping out of school to take a job a junior high school teaching job at Emeryville Middle School in San Francisco. They're gonna pay me $7,500 a year!"

With a furrowed brow and in a fatherly tone he replied, "What? You are going to drop out of school this close to graduation?"

"Yes sir, Dr. Silverman. I have to."

"Listen here, Anthony Burrus. You will *not* drop out of school. I won't allow it," he scolded me.

"But sir," I insisted. "I'm almost 36-years-old and I've been in college for 16 years. I have a wife and child to support. We are poor. You don't understand. We live in the ghetto with an income of $140 a month."

"You want to talk about a ghetto? Have you ever heard of Auschwitz, Belzec, Dachau, and Treblinka? (All are World War II Nazi concentration camps. In Auschwitz alone 1.1 million people were exterminated in four and a half years. One million of them were Jewish men.) Believe me, Anthony Burrus; I *do know* a thing or two about ghettos."

He continued, "Burrus, you will not check out of this institution. I won't allow it."

To me, at the time, it was another white versus black confrontation—a standoff. I thought, *this white man is not gonna tell me that I can't check out. I've gotta drop out."*

"Anthony Burrus, you are a first rate teacher and one day you are going to realize it. You are *not* going to drop out. If you go to the administration to drop out, I will fight every move you make. You can go to the highest authority and I'll be there! *You will not drop out...you will get your degree,* and you'll be a wonderful teacher."

Although I didn't like it when he told me what I *wasn't* going to do, that *white Jewish professor* loved me

74

enough *in spite of my color* to confront me firmly. He challenged me to stand on my feet and be a man; to stay in school until I graduated. I love him and thank him for that today. He affected the rest of my life.

Not long afterward, I received another offer from Dr. George Marr's school at Emeryville, California for a lifetime teaching position with full credentials. However, because of Dr. Marvin Silverman's influence, I passed up that offer as well.

In my 16th year in college, the year before I graduated, I received a call from Dr. Pedrolli, who was in charge of student employment. "Mr. Burrus, we have a job for you as a work-study student. You'll be able to work *and* attend college. I think you qualify. Do you have a driver's license?"

"Yes sir, Dr. Pedrolli, I do." I said excitedly.

"Wonderful. The Berkeley Farm dairy company needs a milk truck driver to deliver milk in the mornings. You should be able to handle that. Be sure and call before you go, to make sure someone is in the office."

I called the dairy and told the man who answered the phone, "Hello sir, my name is Anthony Burrus. I understand that you folks have an opening for a milk truck driver."

"Yes, we do. My name is Earl Hardy. I'm the manager here. Can you come over right away?"

I said, "Sir, I can't come immediately or I'll miss my classes. Can I come in the morning?" He agreed.

The next morning, I arrived at the dairy at 7:45 a.m. for my 8:00 a.m. appointment. As I walked in a man walked up and said, "Can I help you?"

"I'm looking for Mr. Earl Hardy," I said.

"I'm Earl Hardy," he answered.

"Sir, I'm Anthony Burrus." I explained. "We talked yesterday afternoon about your job opening for a milk truck driver, and I'm here to fill out an application."

"Young man, you've come to the wrong place. We don't have any job opening." He said.

"But sir, you essentially hired me yesterday on the telephone," I explained.

"No. I spoke with a young college student who speaks seven languages," he said.

"That's me, Mr. Hardy. I'm the one who speaks seven languages."

"Do you have a driver's license?" He asked.

"Absolutely, sir," I said. I reached into my pocket, pulled out my wallet and showed him my license.

He looked at it and said, "Well, alright, come back tomorrow."

I went back six times, and the sixth time I went back he said, "Listen Burrus, I'm sorry. We *did* have a driver position open. But unfortunately the customers on that particular route all left on vacation, so we don't need a driver for that route at this time."

I was told the following day that they hired a milk truck driver. In my bitterness I thought, *if this is integration and democracy, I want none of it.* I'd left Oklahoma to get away from the "Colored Only," and the "Whites Only" signs posted on the hotel, restaurant, and restroom entrances; and on water fountains and swimming pools. But what I had found in California was the same sentiment, just without the signs. I was so angry I couldn't journal it in English. I wrote in Spanish, "This is what I think of democracy. If this is democracy, you keep it. I don't want it." I was so deeply hurt losing that job.

## Chapter Thirteen

# GRADUATING FROM COLLEGE & BITTERNESS

Having spent four years as a student at Contra Costa and twelve years at San Francisco State, I graduated in 1969. One reason it took me so long was because I had purposely avoided taking the Nuclear Physics course. Remember, I honestly believed that only white students could understand and pass courses like that.

As my college graduation approached, I was surprised to receive a notice that read, "Mr. Burrus, we regret to inform you that you have not yet met the requirements for graduation. You must take Nuclear Physics."

I cautiously enrolled in the course, so I could graduate with my class. The funny thing was, I made a B in the class. I thought, "That was simple! Who said I wasn't college material, and would never make it?" I was so proud. In that moment I vowed that I would never tell a child he or she couldn't learn. In fact, out of a class of 4,500 graduating students I was the only black to be inducted into the National Foreign

Language Honor Society. God in heaven did that for me.

During my years student teaching I'd occasionally have white students who determined that they didn't have to do the homework I assigned them because I was a black teacher. They even said, "We don't have to obey you because you're a black teacher." One of them actually told me, "Daddy said I don't have to write the paper you assigned to me on Dr. M. L. King because he was black."

I've often heard it said of racial reconciliation that we need to build bridges, not bombs. But I disagree. We need not spend time building bridges. The Bridge to connect us has already been built. That Bridge is the person of the Lord Jesus Christ, Son of God! He is our Bridge to each other and to the Heavenly Father!

One day, I realized that one reason I had such difficulty learning was because my heart and mind were so filled with hatred. That day I walked out into the park in front of our home, knelt on the ground, and prayed, "Dear God, please take this hatred out of my heart." I didn't think about asking Him to replace it with anything. I just wanted to be free from the hatred.

Our loving Father took the hatred from my heart and gave me His love for all people. I've been "hatred-free" so long I've almost forgotten how to hate another person. I only hate Satan, sin, sickness, sadness and sorrow.

He gave me so much love, that it caused me some trouble from the other side. I had black friends complain, "Man, you love white people more than you do your own people." But, when God gives you His love for people, you just love people—all colors and flavors of people are "your own people."

I've learned that favor and bitterness can't grow in the same soil. If you allow hatred to control your mind, you limit yourself mentally, socially, spiritually and even economically. You cut off the flow of your blessings.

Someone once said, "Hatred is like drinking poison and praying that it will kill the person you hate!" Bitterness will always do more damage to the vessel in which it's stored than to the person on which it's poured. I cannot count the blessings that have come my way as a result of my allowing His love to displace and dethrone the hatred in my heart.

In the 1990's I was renting a place to live for $1,150 a month in Hercules, California, which is north of Richmond, when one day, I felt God tell me to take my rent money and go to Chicago.

So, I temporarily borrowed $1,150 of my landlord's rent and went to Chicago. While in Chicago I began to teach children in a large warehouse how to count in Chinese and Japanese using some cardboard boxes.

With my head down focusing on what I was doing, surrounded by the children as they counted, I heard someone say, "There he is."

I looked up and saw a lady and her husband walk through the back door. The lady pointed at me and said to the man, "There he is. That's him."

I stopped and welcomed them in, and they asked abruptly, "Sir, how much money do you need?"

I was floored. I couldn't think, much less speak. The wife said, "Well, since you can't tell us how much you need, my husband and I will decide for you." They looked at each other, smiled and said, "We have a figure in mind." With that, they wrote a check for $1,000 and said, "Here, take this. This is what God said for us to give to you."

Later, as we walked down a long hall at the *Institute in Basic Life Principles* I heard a man say, "Excuse me, what is your name?" I stopped, backed up, and looked into the room we'd just passed, and a white man asked, "What is your name and what do you do?"

I said, "My name is Anthony Burrus. I plant the love of God in the hearts of the little children, so that when they grow up, and the devil knocks on the door of their hearts peddling his lies, the light of God's truth will drive him away."

The white man replied, "Well, I would like to have a hand in your ministry."

Then he asked, "What are your needs?" I certainly didn't want to admit that I had a need. So, I replied, "Oh, sir, my family and I are doing fine. We're just fine. We just have a couple of bills, but they are nothing we can't handle, thank you."

He asked again, "What are your needs?"

And again I answered, "We can handle it, Sir. As I said, we just have one or two bills to cover."

He stood up, faced me, and spoke sternly, "Brother, *what* specifically do you need!?"

It was hard for me to tell a white man, who had asked three times about our needs, that we were broke. But I haltingly said, "Well, sir, we're broke. We borrowed our landlord's rent money to come here to Chicago to teach children. We're broke, and we don't have any transportation. Our car caught on fire and burned up."

He said, "Go home and find any car you want to drive. When you do, send me the bill. It's already paid for."

"What else do you need?" he asked.

I said, "We need a movie camera to document our work. Uh, that's all."

He said, "Don't you need a movie screen to shoot it on?"

I said, "Yes, sir."

He said, "Fine, I'll throw in a screen. I just bought a brand new movie camera for my children at Christmas. That's done. Now, what else do you need?"

I said, "Uh, that's it."

He said, "Well, go home and find a car that will suit your needs, and send me the bill. I'll send you the money to pay for it."

As we left for home, he wrote a check to cover our rent. Once we arrived, we shopped and bargained with a salesman for a beautiful Dodge Ram Captain Covered SUV for $5,500. I said, "Man, can you come down $300 more on that price?" I didn't even realize that I was that tight.

He said, "Sure. So he came down to $5,200." I said, "Sold." I sent our benefactor the invoice and he in turn sent me a check for $5,200 to pay for it. We drove that car for three or four years.

In July of 1993, we were in Knoxville, Tennessee at the Thompson-Boling Arena teaching Russian to a class of 5,000 young people. We broke for lunch and walked from the Russian classroom to the cafeteria when two large white hands grabbed my wife and me. One hand was placed my shoulder, and the other hand on my wife's shoulder, and a man said, "Could you all use $1,000?" My wife said, "Yes, we could. Our daughter is about to get married." We looked back to see that it was the white man who'd provided us with our car.

84

He said, "Follow me."

We went to his room where he sat down and wrote a check in our names for $1,000 and said, "There it is."

God has blessed us time after time. He hasn't just opened doors for us. He's blown the hinges off a few of them; and in some cases, he's blown the walls clean off! We continually thank Him for blessing us. If I had continued to embrace my racist hate-filled bitter heart, I am absolutely convinced that those doors never would have opened.

One day I was walking down the hall at Emeryville High School, in Emeryville, California, where as chairman of the Foreign Language Department, I was teaching Spanish when I received a phone call from Dr. Bill Gothard, who at the time was founder and president of the *Institute in Basic Life Principles*.

"Brother Burrus," Bill said. "We would like for you to come to Indianapolis, Indiana and train 300 American English teachers how to teach English to Russian children."

I said, "Alright."

So Dr. Gothard flew me to Indianapolis to teach. One day, at one of the breaks, a brother extended both of his hands and grabbed me by my wrists, as if to see if I was wearing a watch.

I wasn't. I didn't even own a watch. Discovering that, he gave me his $625 watch and said, "My wife and children bought me this watch. I asked for and received their permission to give it to you."

Those 300 teachers went to Russia and began to teach what the Lord had allowed me to teach them. There, Dr. Lubov Kezina, Moscow's Superintendent of Public Instruction said, "Where did you folks ever learn to teach like that?"

They said, "Brother Anthony Burrus taught us."

She said, "Do not dare come back to Russia unless you bring that man with you."

Along with this mission trip to Russia, I've been privileged to participate in trips to New Zealand in 1991; Peru in 2006; to Guadalajara, Mexico in 2008; and to Canada in 2014.

## Chapter Fourteen

# TO THE NATIONS

One day Dr. Gothard called the school where I was teaching again, asking if I would travel to Moscow, Russia to teach English to Russian students.

I asked my superintendent, Dr. John H. Handy if I should leave my school for that period of time.

He answered, "Anthony, this is a once in a lifetime opportunity. I would take it if I were you."

So, I flew to Moscow where the heads of the Russian Education Department opened their schools and gave me carte blanche. "You must speak to our students," they pleaded. I had the opportunity to teach English and preach the Word of God to the students several times. The Russian Education Department had 92 million pupils in their system at the time.

The first school where I taught was an elementary school hidden deep in the woods. It looked to me like an old rusty barn with 20 foot tall doors. I was told the schools were built to withstand American bombs. When we walked inside the teachers said (in Russian), "We've been waiting for you, American. Come in."

"Follow us," the eager teachers motioned. I followed the grandma-like teachers up a winding staircase, struggling to keep up with them. These elderly women walked fast! Trust me, these old folks would've out walked you!

When we arrived at the top floor, they opened the door to a classroom filled with precious Russian children. I asked Dr. Bill, "Now what do you want me to do?"

He said, "Just be you. Teach over here like you do in your own school."

As we stepped into the room, the teacher said (in Russian), "Stand up, children."

Without a moment's hesitation those twenty-five children snapped obediently to attention. I thought, *wow, these kids need to come and teach some of our students about discipline.*

Then the teacher ordered, "Sit down," and they sat down at attention.

I stepped up and exclaimed, "Good morning!" (in Russian).

They replied, "Good morning."

I said (in English), "Good morning. How are you? Do you speak English?"

I had such fun talking with them in Russian and with the few English phrases they learned. They were fascinated to hear about America, and very excited to learn our language.

However, no one had prepared me for what happened next.

The children in this fourth grade class were quite small. I knelt down in front of a little blonde Russian boy and said softly, "Boy, what is your name?"

He replied, "My name is Dima."

I looked into little Dima's eyes and said sincerely in his Russian language, "Dima, Dima, I love you very, very much."

Dima's eyes remained fixed on mine for a moment, until tears filled his bright eyes, and began cascading down his rosy cheeks. I turned to the next child.

"What is your name?" I asked him.

"My name is Vladimir Dubrowsky," he replied. With his eyes locked on mine, I said to him in Russian, words that he'd never heard. "Vladimir Dubrowsky, I love you very, very much." I went down the rows, telling this to each child, then leaving those students in tears, I'd move to another classroom.

After I completed one floor of classrooms, I was led down to the next floor. Before long, students throughout the whole building were weeping.

I suppose you could have followed me that day by the trail of tears. Kids in every classroom I visited were crying. I finally asked, "Why are all of these children crying behind me?"

One of my hosts explained, "Brother Burrus, in Russia it's against the law for parents to tell their children they love them. These children have never heard anyone tell them that they are loved."

I said, "Really? That's so hard for me to conceive. We do that automatically in America."

I was shocked to discover that in their culture (at least at that time) to tell a child you love him was to admit that you were insane. For that, you'd be placed in an institution and administered drugs. They had never been told they were loved.

Next they had me address their college students. At the conclusion of my speech, I said, "I love you. May I give each of you a hug before I leave?"

They too were shocked and began to whisper among themselves. I realized that they were debating quietly whether or not I would actually do that.

"He wouldn't dare. He's a professor. Professors don't do that," they whispered.

I held up a little bottle of anointing oil and said, "Come." As they did, I anointed each of them with a drop of that wonderfully scented oil and gave each a hug. As I hugged those Russian children, I could feel their little bodies tremble under the power and presence of God flowing through me. I simply loved those kids like I did my own children. One by one they walked back to their seats wiping peaceful tears of joy from their eyes.

Then one of the teachers said (in Russian), "What about us? Don't forget us."

"Form a line," I replied (in Russian). Then I anointed and hugged each of the teachers too, and the same thing happened.

One precious young lady said, "You know, Mr. Burrus, if I could imagine God, He would look just like you. He would have beautiful black skin just like yours." Later I spoke in a large auditorium, and as I spoke, I overheard a discussion about me (in Russian).

One girl said, "He could not be an American because Americans hate us."

Another replied, "There isn't a bone of hate in his body. That man loves everyone."

A third insisted, "He is not an American!"

"Yes, he is!"

"No, he isn't!"

"Yes, he is!"

At the conclusion of my speech, the most outspoken among them, a young lady, made a special request to sit down and have lunch with me. I agreed.

The lunch was arranged at historic Colonel Vladimir's Palace in St. Petersburg, built in the late 1800s.

She sat and stared at me in disbelief. In Russian she said, "American. Where I come from they teach us that you Americans believe that if all Russians were annihilated, there would be no more problems in the world. Just kill all the Russians and eliminate all the problems."

The other Russian kids responded, "That's what we're taught about Americans."

They studied me and finally said, "You are an American. We are Russian. Someone has lied to us. You don't hate us. How then can we hate you? We don't hate you, American."

Everyone, at our table, both the Russians and our American team wept as we left the table. We left families in Russia that we love very much.

Before long, word spread from building to building, and city to city. People were saying, "We want to meet the American who makes children cry with the forbidden words."

Love truly transcends all racial boundaries, all borders and politics. Love knows no bounds.

● ● ●

On October 17, 2001 I received a package in the mail from New Zealand. It was a New Zealand textbook, "Teach Yourself Maori."

Around 7:00 p.m. that evening I sat down at our dinner table, opened the book, and in less than an hour God gave me the entire sound and grammatical structure of the Maori language.

I jumped up from the table and ran to tell my wife, "I got it, Honey. God has given me the phonetics and morphology of the entire Maori language!" College didn't teach me that. *God did that for me!*

Soon after that, Dr. Bill Gothard called long distance and asked me to open his New Zealand Basic Seminar in the Maori Language. I'd assured him that I would. So we boarded a 747 intercontinental jetliner headed for New Zealand.

At one point, Drew Tillman yelled from the rear of the plane, "Anthony, when are you going to speak some Maori for us?"

I said, "I will do so as soon as we land in New Zealand and I breathe some fresh Maori air."

"You've got six Maori women sitting right behind you," Drew said.

Sure enough, there were six women wrapped in blankets seated on the row behind me. I turned to them and timidly said in pure Maori, "Excuse me. I'm trying to learn to speak Maori. Would you help me with pronunciation?"

With that, all of the women jumped to attention and threw back their blankets as though they'd been poked with a cattle prod. "Who is your teacher?" one asked.

I said, "God is teaching me."

She said, "Your pronunciation is perfect. You don't need any help at all."

As requested, I opened the seminar in the Maori language. 10,000 people rose to their feet to see the black American who could speak their language.

God has blessed me with the gift of languages to reach His people all over the world.

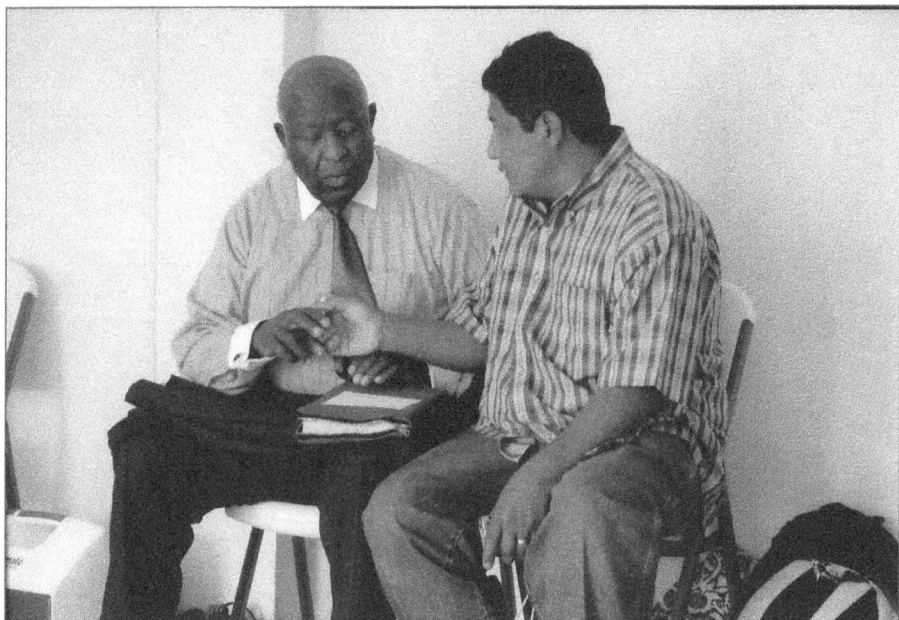

## Chapter Fifteen
# MEETING JESUS PHYSICALLY

In 2010 a group of Texas doctors at Providence Hospital in Waco sawed my chest open, reached in, took my heart out and cut on it. Then they attached a piece of artery from my leg to it, placed my heart back inside my chest, and sewed me up!

The medication administered to me for surgery caused me to hear the beating of my own heart. It wasn't the gentle thump, thump, I'd heard before. My heart was pounding like a jackhammer. Suddenly the level of pain in my chest was off the charts. On a scale of 1-10, my pain level was about 27 and climbing! As I lay on that hospital bed, I suddenly felt myself falling down, down—straight down. It felt as if I was falling one million miles a second, down into a dark foreboding place.

Suddenly I was surrounded by what appeared to be 10,000 black octopus-looking demons tormenting me, calling out, "Come, come, come, come..." Suddenly a little white line appeared and I heard one say, "Step over the white line and we'll stop your pain." My pain was excruciating. but I knew in my heart that I was not to cross the line.

The demon speaking urged me more forcefully saying, "Come, come, come. Step over the line." And then what felt like thousands of them behind me began me, urging me, "Go on, go on, step across the line and your pain will end." Everywhere I looked, the nasty creatures were shouting, "Come on. Step over the white line, and we'll drop your pain level. It's easy—simple. Come on."

The pain was more excruciating by the moment. My heart was throbbing, pounding, but I wasn't about to cross that white line. For some reason, I knew that to do so would spell disaster. All I could do was lie there and hurt as my pain level increased more and more.

It was then that I found the presence of mind to speak four simple words. I had been so distracted by and focused on the pain that the thought hadn't crossed my mind. I said, *"Help me, Lord Jesus."* The second those words crossed my lips, Jesus appeared. There, standing in my room was Jesus, the Son of God! Everything in the entire room became bathed in brilliant light.

Every demon instantly vanished in the glow of His Presence, and my pain level began to drop dramatically. As long as He stood there my pain level subsided. It became clear to me that the white line had been a deception. Had I stepped over it I would have denied Jesus.

That, friend, is one thing that I'll never do. Don't ever deny Jesus. He brought me back from the halls of hell, from the den of death, in answer to four little words, *"Help me, Lord Jesus."* I dared to call on my heavenly Daddy. Whatever you are facing today, call on Him. He will hear and answer you.

## Chapter Sixteen

# SOME CRUMBS FROM THE GOLDEN LOAF

I was on the phone talking with a Christian brother who goes by the name John 3:16 in Tennessee.

He said, "Our friend Bill has no income. I'm going to send him a check for $10,000 by 9:00 a.m. tomorrow morning."

The next morning John 3:16 called to tell me that he'd sent the $10,000 as promised.

I said, "John, allow me to pray a Deuteronomy 1:11 blessing over you." I did. Deuteronomy 1:11 says, *"May the LORD, the God of your ancestors, increase you a thousand times and bless you as he has promised!"*

Three weeks later I flew to Chicago for an international board meeting of the *Institute in Basic Life Principles*. One of the first people I saw when I arrived was John 3:16. I went over to him and asked, "Brother John, did that Deuteronomy 1:11 blessing that I prayed over you work?"

He said, "Yes. I'm going home to collect my first monthly check for more than one million dollars." God had given him ten million dollars!

I saw him recently in Nashville, Tennessee. John 3:16 pledged a million dollars to help a widow with eleven children!

I prayed this blessing over a contractor. God is blessing him mightily. While in Chicago I blessed an unemployed man named Bill. Last week Bill said that God blessed him with so much until he gave a thousand dollars to another needy person, and had blessed more than 3,000 people during the past 28 days!

On October 9th, 2013, a Spanish speaking pastor from Guinea, Southwest Africa shared his need with our congregation. God spoke to my heart and said, "Give this pastor $100 dollars." I happily obeyed. Then God said, "Give him another $100 dollars."

Now I had been dreaming of buying a 1999 four-door Lincoln Town Car that I had found. It was a beauty and was on sale for $2,500. I had a jar at home which held $260 dollars toward my dream car. In spite of my hopeful savings jar, my wife rained on my parade saying, "Honey, don't buy that Lincoln."

I was disappointed and discouraged, as if God had forgotten me. Then I heard God say, "Empty your Lincoln jar. Give the $250 dollars to the African pastor."

I immediately began to remind God that I was now officially broke, and that I had recently given my faithful 1983 Fleetwood Brougham Cadillac to another Christian brother in need. I didn't want to give my money too, but I did.

Now I was both "car-less" and broke. Two nights later at midnight our doorbell rang. *What do they want this time? Money? We're broke.* I sighed inwardly.

My wife opened the door, stepped outside, put her hands to her face as tears filled her eyes. "Honey, come here." Not knowing what might have happened I rushed outside.

A gold 2005, 4-door Lincoln Signature Town car gleamed in the moonlight, while my daughter grinned from ear-to-ear.

She and her husband said, "Go ahead, get in! Drive it and enjoy Mother and Daddy!"

Whenever we hold a seed in our hand, we should remember that God's got a harvest on His mind. The harvest is later than when the seed is sown; and will always be greater than the seed sown.

The seeds we sow never really leave our lives. Instead, when they leave our hands they travel into our future to create a great harvest. *Don't be stingy!*

The grace of God will always empower us to do what the Word of God commands. In Luke 6:38 we are commanded to give. God made a covenant with us saints. When we give, He gives back to us in the same measure as we gave. If we give generously, God rewards us generously. If we give stingily, He returns to us the same.

However, if we give a good measure (generously), God will cause men to give us a good measure, pressed down, and shaken together.

I love this biblical formula. According to Deuteronomy 1:11, when we give five dollars to the poor, to a widow, to the sick or someone in need, God matches our gift 1,000 to one!

Similarly, in Mark 10:30 God promises to match every dollar we give with $100 dollars in this life.

In Genesis 26:12-13 we read of Isaac's gift, *"Isaac planted crops in that land and the same year reaped a hundredfold, because the* LORD *blessed him.* [13] *The man became rich, and his wealth continued to grow until he became very wealthy."*

Finally, in Psalms 115:13-14 we are told, *"He* (God) *will bless those who fear the LORD-- small and great alike. May the LORD make you increase, both you and your children."* Clearly it is God's heart to bless us. However, stingy givers either don't understand this, or they don't trust God, which is foolish.

- Give to feed the poor.
- Support to the *Jewish Voice Ministries,* International at http://www.jewishvoice.org/
- Give to the *International Fellowship of Christians and Jews* at http://www.ifcj.org

# Shalom Yeshua Hamashia!

Reverend Anthony Burrus

## Chapter Seventeen

# IN CONCLUSION

Years ago, three men died on crosses on a hill called Golgotha, on the outskirts of the city of Jerusalem. One of them *lost his life*. One *found his life*, and the Man in the middle *gave His life*. Let's lay down our lives for each other. (John 15:13) Let's stop shunning each other because of the color of our skin. In the past, we've said, "How are you doing?" at a distance. We've loved at a distance. We've prayed for one another at a distance.

It's time that we reach out and take our brother by his hand, and walk over that bridge into this world and meet the needs we see.

● ● ●

One day a young man named Mark Andre walked up to me and did something that the Supreme Court cannot do. Mark and another man looked me in the eyes and said, "Brother Burrus, I want you to forgive me for what my ancestors did to your people." With those words, walls I'd built inside my heart, walls of fear, hatred and bitterness fell. They've never been, nor never will be rebuilt. You think the Berlin Wall's collapse was something? What happened inside of me that day was greater. I hugged Mark and we cried. It felt good, because God has set us free!

Today my heart is light, my spirit is even lighter, and my hope is beyond that. It's not about who is right, about civil rights, or even about equal rights. His *real* challenge is for us to *do what is right!*

As I conclude this book in 2014, I'm pleased to report that Heri, our daughter still owns her beauty shop in Waco. Our son Enzi isn't married. He is a graduate of Sequoia Institute of Technology in Fremont, California as a certified ASE mechanic, and serves as minister of music at Greater Mount Olive Baptist Church where his brother-in-law is pastor, and his sister Enda is first lady. Our first-born son, Larry Burrus, is a licensed California contractor.

www.ingramcontent.com/pod-product-compliance
Lightning Source LLC
Chambersburg PA
CBHW021828090426
42811CB00032B/2074/J